Steam Laundry

Steam Laundry

poems by

Nicole Stellon O'Donnell

borealbooks

Steam Laundry
Copyright © 2012 by Nicole Stellon O'Donnell
All rights reserved

Book design and layout by Andrew Mendez

ISBN 978-1-59709-228-9
Library of Congress Catalog Card Number: 2011942739

The Los Angeles County Arts Commission, the National Endowment for the Arts, and Los Angeles Department of Cultural Affairs partially support Red Hen Press.

Boreal Books is an imprint of Red Hen Press
www.borealbooks.org
First Edition

Acknowledgments

"Mother-in-law" and "Lost Luxury" appeared in *The Women's Review of Books*. "Infidelity," "River Town," and "Raven" appeared in *Cirque: A Literary Journal for the North Pacific Rim*.

I'm grateful to the University of Alaska Fairbanks Archives for their assistance and patience. Special thanks to Caroline, Anne, and Rose for all the time they put into helping me with my research.

I'd like to thank Theresa Bakker for striking the match. Thanks to Chris Allan, Melina Draper, Sarah Doetschman, and Joeth Zucco for their readings and comments. Special thanks to TJ O'Donnell for reading and rereading again.

Special thanks to Peggy Shumaker for her encouragement and support.

Sincere thanks to the Rasmuson Foundation, who supported the writing of this book with an Individual Artist Project Award. Their generosity gave me the gift of time to write.

Finally, I send gratitude to Sarah Ellen Gibson, Elmer Gibson, Tom Gibson, Will Butler, Joe Gibson, and Hannah Mullen for letting me shrug on the overcoats of their lives for a spell. I am especially grateful to Tom Gibson for saving every letter, receipt, photograph, and calling card that came his way over the years. As I imagine it's difficult to have someone borrow your life, Mr. Gibson, with deep respect, I'll misquote you, "You will have to excuse this writing, as the poetry is rough and the pencil runs away with itself."

Photo Citations

Page 13, Sarah Ellen Gibson Collection, Accession Number 59-804-161, Archives, Alaska and Polar Regions Collections, Rasmuson Library, University of Alaska Fairbanks.

Page 61, Sarah Ellen Gibson Collection, Accession Number 59-804-001, Archives, Alaska and Polar Regions Collections, Rasmuson Library, University of Alaska Fairbanks.

Page 70, Sarah Ellen Gibson Collection, Accession Number 59-804-182, Archives, Alaska and Polar Regions Collections, Rasmuson Library, University of Alaska Fairbanks.

Page 86, Sarah Ellen Gibson Collection, Accession Number 59-804-160, Archives, Alaska and Polar Regions Collections, Rasmuson Library, University of Alaska Fairbanks.

Page 102, Sarah Ellen Gibson Collection, Accession Number 78-76-44, Archives, Alaska and Polar Regions Collections, Rasmuson Library, University of Alaska Fairbanks.

Page 111, Sarah Ellen Gibson Collection, Accession Number 59-804-150, Archives, Alaska and Polar Regions Collections, Rasmuson Library, University of Alaska Fairbanks.

Page 136, Sarah Ellen Gibson Collection, Accession Number 59-804-137, Archives, Alaska and Polar Regions Collections, Rasmuson Library, University of Alaska Fairbanks.

Table of Contents

—for TJ

—for Cedar and Coral

Steam Laundry

Author's Note

In 1896 Sarah Ellen Gibson followed her husband, Joe, to San Francisco so he could pursue a job as a fireman on the railroad. In 1898 she followed him to Dawson City, Yukon Territory, in the first Klondike stampede of the gold rush. In 1903 she left for Alaska in the first wave of stampeders after gold was discovered in the hills outside of Fairbanks. These poems tell her story. While all the characters are real people and the events depicted are true, I've taken liberties to fill in the narrative and emotional gaps. In some of the poems, found phrases and lines are taken directly from the letters and documents; others are wholly products of my imagination.

River Town

The men who became street names
meet in a saloon in the afterlife.

They raise glasses, clink. Whiskey spills over the lip
and onto their dirty fingers. They smile

and nod, bob their heads in the only agreement
they've ever all shared:

it's a pleasure to see the roads they cut
through stands of willow paved.

Whether they're in heaven, surrounded by dance hall girls,
straps falling over shoulders,

or they're in hell, sweating in starched paper collars,
bones aching with regret, they're still with us,

perched on poles, peeking out between
the loops and columns of the letters on their names.

The two brothers-in-law who intersect
at the library and the Korean restaurant

watch a man jaywalk, wondering if he ever sold out a partner,
or brought a bank to ruins.

The bank president looks down from his corner
onto run-down apartments.

On Saturday nights, cruiser lights reflect off him,
as men in handcuffs shuffle through the winter's first snow.

The rent collector snakes from First to Third, disappearing
before Fifth. On that street, everyone locks their doors.

When a boy jumps his bike over a curb, and looks up,
he thinks he hears faint applause.

And the woman signaling left on Isabelle feels an inescapable
longing as the tick of the turn signal counts out

her heartbeats, as if she had to sneak out of town
in the middle of winter in a sled, hands clasped in a wolf fur muff.

All of them wish they could climb back down, muddy
their feet on the riverbank, but the afterlife, if anything,

is green and reflective, and perfectly still,
unlike the river, which so long after they bottomed out,

is still going the same brown direction.

Almost Anagram

—Fairbanks Camp, Chena River, Alaska, 1903

Even before I was born,
my mother named me Sarah Ellen.
She thought first of her grandmother,
Sarah, stern and tightly laced
in the frowning gray of a photograph;
then of her sister, Ellen,
dead in childhood,
all sweetness and eyelet lace,

and she decided,
her grandmother's name, Sarah,
being too big for a baby,
she would call me Ellen,
and I would carry Sarah,
out in front like a farmhouse porch,
so everyone outside could see,
while in the parlor,
the name Ellen would bring her sister
back into the world.

But months later, seeing my first smile
come forth without dimples,
and smoothing the black shine
of my hair, too unlike
the blonde baby curls of her sister,
she decided she would call me by another name.

She turned the letters around—Ellen to Nellie,
a quilt repatched, both old and new,
but not quite the little girl
she mourned once on the porch
as her mother wept inside.
When she held her breath,
the hardness of the wooden chair
bit into the backs of her knees.
Each time her mother screamed,
the curtains blew out over the sill
as if the house was breathing grief.

So when years later, me,
the girl named for grief,
and renamed, was married,
the preacher said, *Nellie,
do you take this man,*
and I said, *I do.* I being
an almost anagram of the girl
my mother imagined me to be.

With that marriage ending,
I rearrange the letters again
and return to Ellen, the lost blonde girl.
Her feet swinging happily at the back
of the wagon as she sang
her way out of town.

Correspondence: A Recommendation

—*Ontario, Canada, June 7, 1896*

To Whom it may Concern.

This is to certify that Joseph Gibson has been employed as a fireman on Ontario Division of the Canadian Pacific Railroad since the month of October 1894 to present. He has discharged his duties most satisfactorily and I cheerfully recommend him to any one in want of such a person.

He has been a sober, intelligent, and trustworthy man with practical experience to qualify him in my opinion to take charge of an engine anytime.

He leaves this division for duty near the Pacific Coast on Canadian Pacific Railroad.

Signed,

M. A. Mirkby
Lead Fireman

In the House of Our New Marriage

—San Francisco, 1896

Once, you lay
your head on my lap
and listened to me read:

I am the rose of Sharon,
and the lily of the valleys.

My left hand rearranged
your hair against the folds of my skirt,
and, with my fingertips, I mapped
the day's heat
across your scalp.

The book's weight
in my right hand,
the dust in the air,
the honey of my breath,
a murmur:

for thy love is better than wine.

Our marriage was so new
I could hold it in my palm
like an egg still warm
from the henhouse.

I thought of the egg,
a white promise,

and forgot the hen's loss,
the shards of shell.

Once, sweetly,
you lay your head in my lap
and listened to me read:

love is as strong as death
jealousy is as cruel as the grave

from the only book we had
under the beams and rafters
in the newly raised house
of our marriage.

Wife, I Ask You Once More

—July 20, 1897, San Francisco
after the news of the Klondike gold discoveries began to spread

I confess the saloon
has swallowed our marriage,
Faro taken too dear a price.
In this city, so far from our families,
I have broken promises,
and dishes, and windows.

I didn't think I'd be the kind of man I've become,

but Nellie, I was on the dock the day the *Excelsior*
steamed into San Francisco carrying
men who dug their freedom from a gold vein.
They stood on the deck, gaping,
as the throng called out and desire
fogged the air. I stood,
one in an ocean of hats, so crowded,
that there was nowhere for the rich men
to climb off.

Then, I read about the *Portland*'s landing in Seattle.
A Ton of Gold the newspaper said.
Share enough for any man willing to dig.

Tommie watched with me.
In his eyes, I glimpsed what I once was,
the boy who first followed you

the distance of a picket fence,
and later asked you to follow me,
and the railroad, my livelihood,
to this coast.

And that boy led me
to remember you,
the girl, looking up from her psalm book
in the dark polished pew.

I will go after a new life
if you will follow and bring our boys.
We can bury the past under tailings.

The neighbors crowd the outfitters
anxious to get grub, to sack and crate,
drag and freight.

Wife, will you follow?
Will you wait?

Like Skin

We like to think there are two kinds:
those who leave and those left behind.

There, men grind a life out of dirt,
haul it up.
They either fold bank notes
into envelopes and send
them home,

or they don't.

Here, women, all boot buttons and business,
write letters and wait
with children playing on the porch,

or without.

But anyone can buy a ticket, lean
into the steamer's rail, breathe
in wood smoke and wait.

Anyone can hide a pen in a pocket,
and never lift it to write,
unwilling to beg even paper.

Anyone can heft a cast iron skillet,
melt butter, crack eggs.

And anyone can knead dough,
fold it onto itself
until like skin,
it barely yields to the touch.

Chilkoot Trail

—San Francisco to Dawson City, Yukon Territory, 1897

August 14, Portland

Dear Nellie,

I have a bad pen; excuse the haste.
On the way to the Klondike,
waiting is my occupation.
Rumors scratch the days
and chew the minutes.

When we leave depends
on when she gets her freight
aboard. Her freight is us and our outfits.
We are ready to board, yet the weight
of our gear holds us up.
All day we lift and load:
sacks, tools, lumber.

Each man I see has the same scowl,
the same set jaw. Each man folds his arms,
and looks down.

One has new boots.
Another's are worn.
One shifts his weight and looks away.
One has brought a good hat.
One wears wool britches without patches.
One cracks his knuckles and stares at the water.

We shake hands and nod,
firm, stone-eyed.
We lean over the rail and spit.
I know few names,
most nicknames,
some hometowns.

There was rough passage
Wednesday afternoon.
Some were sick,
slumped against the rail,
but I was all right,
so was John and the dog.

Tell Tommie and Elmer
to be good boys. It's time
they learned to do without
their father. When they come
to work the claim I stake,
they'll have enough of me.

Good-bye, Dear Wife,

Joe

Dear Joe,

This morning I snapped out the quilt
over the mattress, and for a second
it stayed suspended, borne only
by my fingertips and air.

If I knew what to say, I'd pull
a page and pen from the desk
and write. Instead I draw in the wash,
sweep this day's dust from the kitchen,
and feed the boys.

On Tuesday, I'll take in more wash,
but I will think of you.
On the trail you will be the grime
that clings to your clothes.

At home, I am the quilt suspended,
the half second before it falls
to the mattress, ripple of patches
and labor, floating above
the sagging, empty bed.

Your wife,

Nellie

August 21, Queen Charlotte Sound

Dear Nellie,

Near the Alaska boundary,
the fog is so thick
we will have to lay here
all night.

The ship pitched so much this morning
that the breakfast table
sat empty of patrons.
Men clung to the rails.
I wavered with them.

The mules, stowed below, are in a good place.
I hear they may not survive the trail.
Barebacked and tethered, they wait
without knowing they wait.

When this ship stops rocking,
men will fold against the rail,
weighted with concern:
steep ascents, wrecked rafts,
dry goods soaked. Even our
imaginations are heavy.

We will reach Dyea about Saturday.
Ready or unready, our walk
will begin there.

Remember me to the boys.

Believe love is a blessing.

Believe I will write again,

Joe

Dear Joe

This morning the fog rolls
off the bay and mutes
the early light in the window.
I can't find you or write you.
Instead with your letter
creased in my lap,
I consider your boys.

At fifteen, Tommie is
so like my father, and Elmer
at thirteen is so like you.

When he ducks his head toward
his bowl at breakfast,
your eyes peer out from under
the blunt cut of his hair.

He holds his spoon like you,
and when he smiles, I expect
your laugh to follow.

I believe. I do,
in the envelope,
in the letter passed
from hand to hand.

I believe you will send for us.

Despite myself, I trust that claim.

Yours,

Nellie

August 23, Fort Wrangell

Dear Nellie,

We reached Wrangell at six this morning.

Fog detained us. Now stopped here
for fresh water, we rise and breathe
as if we belong to this boat.
We cut logs, haul them aboard,
and stack them to feed the engine
before we can move forward.

Every passenger has a partner
and believes he will be
the next to hit pay dirt, that his struggle
will bring gain. There are moments
I wonder how much gold there can be.
There are moments that longing
alone propels this boat.

We are impatient to reach Dyea,
but we'll have enough of walking later.
On the boat, it's out of the question.

I expect to see Juneau this afternoon.
I will write from there.
God knows when I will get
another chance.

They say thousands are hung up at the pass,
but I pay no attention to rumor.
We are going through the worst
right now, or I fear, the best.

All for the present,

Joe

Dear Joe,

I pay some attention to rumor.

I know what the neighbors say,
what gets whispered nights on the other
side of the thin wall.

For every miner, a wife waits.
For every wife, a shot glass.
For every glass, a bartender.
For every bartender, a stool.
For every stool, a petticoat,
a boot heel, a bare knee.

I do pay some attention to rumor.

If women gambled like men,
clutched cards, stared firm
into each other's hardened eyes,
I know what the odds would be on your promises.

But women gamble like women,
so, eyes closed, I wait for your next letter.

Yours,

Nellie

August 26, Skagway

Dear Nellie,

There has been a terrible storm.
We worked night and day
to get the Skagway freight ashore.

We heaved, dragged, and soaked
ourselves in mud, before we even
saw our destination.

On the rocks at Dyea,
men outnumber stones.
The beach is piled with outfits,
grub, canvas-bagged and stacked,
tools teetering atop the mounds.

There is no warehouse, no dock, no ceremony,
just baggage and cussing,
shouts blasting across the water.

Anxious to get the boat turned around
they threw the horses into the water
and let them swim to shore.
The mules and dogs as well.
I watched them bob and struggle,
wild-eyed and snorting.

Skagway measures time in arrivals and departures.
Because there are no days, there is no Sunday,
no rest.

We will start the trail on arrival.
Men tell it is terrible passing.
There are about four hundred people striving
along in White Pass
and over two hundred on the Dyea.

They say White Pass,
just a cut through the woods,
is as much a lie as a trail.
They say the end disappears
like a rumor whispered
too long from ear to ear.
I'll take Dyea.

White Pass, lined with dead horses,
was supposed to be easy,
but clearing the trees and the rain
ruined it. There's so much rain
these past days that the horses sink
to their necks. Corduroy
bridges, log stacked after log
for traction, send more horses,
broken-ankled to their deaths.

I can't describe some of the men
gone clean crazy.
Two from this steamer
have lost their minds.
I long for a camera to record
their eyes, but I suspect,
the loss wouldn't
show through even then.

More are giving up,
turning for home.
Some sell flour for 50 cents a sack,
some burn fuel, and more
are going to winter in Juneau.
Others cut trees, chink logs, and plan
to stay here. I am going on.

When I strike pay dirt,
I will send for you
in June or May.
Tell Elmer to be a good boy,
and tell Tommie to keep that big head
of his well and slick.

This is the last we will be able to send out
until we get moving.

My Love,

Joe

Dear Joe,

That big head of his is the same
and so are all the other boys in town,
after their fathers head north
as they wait for calls to follow.

I don't know what's behind their eyes.
Our sons grow taller and more quiet.
They measure and weigh, think
before speaking. The boys they once were
fade more with each morning's sun.
In the kitchen, they grunt and gulp coffee,
scrape their plates clean. The world is wearing
on them, like all of us.

San Francisco, or the whole coast,
has become a waiting parlor.
Women shift on benches, read papers,
force smiles, fret.
So many men have gone.

In letters, some husbands tell it true,
others polish their words
and set them carefully.
Many don't write at all.
No one here talks about
what you've written me,
about the trails, the rain, the men.

The only reading we admit to each other
is the newspaper, and we imagine the struggle
it will be to carry bags full of gold dust
down from the hills.

Eyes shining, men smile,
buy outfits, and wait on the docks.

They slap each other on the back,
laughing, but in the news the photographers
catch them stern-mouthed, serious, plotting.

It's the Klondike,
not the trail. They don't
even consider the trail.

If there are more men than stones,
there are more men to come.
The beach will be built of their bones before long.

Your wife,

Nellie

September 29, Lake Lindeman

Dear Nellie,

I have been upriver
getting out timber.
The boat will be ready
to launch tomorrow
about noon.

We will start at dawn,
all being well.

The state of affairs on the trail
was past description.
The camps have names:
Sheep Camp, Stone House, Pleasant Camp,
Canyon City, Happy Camp.
A map rewritten would read:
Misery, Distress, Turn Back.

Only those with the most money
or strongest ever
get through it.
I got the grub,
a winter's worth,
over the pass.
I will get through.

Snowing here.
I have been sleeping in my wet
clothes for over a week.
Each morning, flinching, I wring
them out, and, still cold,
pull them on and start the day.

I send out my love for a
dear little wife.

Do not write to me
as you cannot reach me.

I will write as soon as I reach quarters.

We may
get frozen on the river
or stormbound on the lake.
So you may not hear
from me.

Remember me in your prayers.
Write to father and mother.

I am lonesome,

Joe

Dear Joe,

There are objects in this house that have weight,
that ask in their lifting, for a certain effort:

the washtub, the iron kettle, the laundry wringer,
your mother's old skillet.

The boys too, once. Years ago I hefted them
onto my hip, worked single-armed, twisting

to keep them away from the hot stove.
They grew, gained their legs, and I regained

my arms. Underfoot, larger, but less weight
for me to carry, I could go about my work

with them weaving around my skirt, shouting
and singing. They changed and changed me.

If our marriage has a weight, it's not cast iron
or painted china. It's not the shifting slop

of a bucket, or ten pounds of burlap
lumpy with potatoes. It's like our boys, first pink

and wailing, light, sized to be tucked
into the crook of an arm, then heavy,

struggling and clinging. Now they're grown.
They can work and they will leave. Alone, with

you up north, I sew and visit, eavesdrop
on the neighbors' squabbles, and I feel

weightless. When you finally call for us, I will
answer and even follow, but I wonder

if you have really gained your legs. I
wonder if I have the strength to heft

anything more. I am not so lonesome
as I thought I'd be.

Still yours,

Nellie

At Last an Invitation from 13 Eldorado

—Dawson City, Yukon Territory, January 30, 1898

Dearest Nellie,

I am well and still
working on 13 Eldorado,
but you don't know that.
I wrote to you some two months ago.
I just learned the mail had not gone out yet.
My first letter stalled,
maybe this one will find you.

My wife, I see you
at the edge of the harbor.
You shade your eyes
against the sunset.
Hair loose from the twist
at the nape of your neck
waves along your cheek.

You think I am gone,
not thinking of you,
lost to the ice and mud.
You think I am one of those
men, and wait for a letter,
envelope framed in black. Inside
a stranger's script might read
faithful, strong, hard worker,
tragedy, now with his Lord.

But I am nowhere near God,
unless God is an axe or a shovel.
When I lose myself,
I think of you,
our home, the worn carpet,
the sharp smell of soap,
the dent on the coffeepot's handle.
I know the cracked
walls of the apartment,
the window, paint
chipping from the panes.
I know the creak
of the third step from
the top of the stairs.
Coming in too late,
I regret to admit
I used to skip that step.

Now, it's time I sent for you again.

Here is what I want you to do. Come up
the Yukon by St. Michael.
Not the way I came.
Go to the Alaska Commercial Company office
soon as you get this letter.
Take a man along with you,
for passage will be hard to get.
Be sure to get a man who speaks well

and is known to the agent.
He can tell the company
they will get the money
through their store at Dawson.

If you cannot bring grub with you, come without it,
but bring bedding and clothes
and your sewing machine.
Bring the clothes wringer.
Bring your thread and needle.
Put everything in canvas covering.
Keep the packs from getting too heavy,
as you will be at the whim of the men
handling the freight.
Don't dare owe anyone favors.

I will not likely be in town when you come.
You can find where I am
at the Alaska Commercial Company store
or from Tom O'Brien at the Klondike Lily
one mile from Dawson. I promise that
if you walk it, it will be the last mile
I ever ask of you.
I promise I will try and have a cabin
in town for you. If not, I have a big
tent at Tom O'Brien's.

Keep this letter and it will identify you.
Send word by freighter to me,

and O'Brien will see that some reliable man
gets your message to me on the claim.

Some reliable man, that's the rub.
Even John and Charlie sold out the grub
while I was ahead building the boat at Lindeman.
All out of fear of soaking.
I hauled all that over the pass.
I lifted and pulled, then, without consult,
my partners unburdened themselves of my labor,
my winter's cache. They feared the forming ice,
the crush from the banks, the creak of the gunwales.
To them, water was more fearsome than a boss,
but I feared working another man's claim,
and I find myself working another man's claim.

The men trail through the streets,
unrecognizable puffs and bundles.
We raise our arms to acknowledge
what smolders inside each wool coat,
but we don't stop to speak.

I will tell you the truth.
The trails to the dance halls and saloons
are worn deepest. Other men's boots smooth
and carve out the edges after each new snow,
so you may wonder,
but come.

I am a changed man.
I can tell you no strangers for me anymore.

I could have $1,000 when you get here.
I will work and get lots of grub together.
If the boys can get a dog team and hunt
and you take in laundry again,
the three of you can make more than me.
If we get a claim, we can get enough
together in a couple of years
to get a home some place and be somebody.

I am a changed man, Nellie.
No swigs, no skirts, no late nights.
The candles in my tent have burned down,
flames winking as I lay on the cot
staring at the grainy canvas.

Elmer, my little man, on the boat
keep near your mother and do not worry her
and I will be very proud of you.
Tommie, you will be the man now.
Remember your mother in all your decisions.

Nellie, when you find me
in the yellowed fall light
I will be very proud of you.
On the boat, take your advice from a good source.

Even though they are now too old, kiss the boys for me.
I have lovely whiskers that you won't recognize.

Good-bye, darling. Have a start.
I have had one, and beginning is the best part.

Your husband,

Joe

Correspondence: Receipt for Freight

—San Francisco, June 1898

3 Steuart Street.

San Francisco. JUN 1 1898

Mrs Nellie Gibson & 2 boys   Tickets 16 B 1572-1573

In account with   Alaska-Yukon Transportation Co.

(13)

Freight on 56 pkgs sundries

22 weight   1150
34 meas^{mt}   95'8"
less all^{ce} on 2 Tickets 2000 lbs
= 3933 lbs @ 5¢   196 65
State Tolls   25
                    196 90

PAID
JUN 1 1898
ALASKA YUKON TRANSP'N CO.

The Younger Brother Speaks

—On the Yukon, Summer 1898

I watch Tommie slanting himself toward the water
as we steam upriver,
cap dirty, bent at the waist.
He leans his elbows into the rail.

There is only two years between us,
but it's a long stretch, maybe as long
as the stretch of this river, beginning
in one country and spilling out in another.

My brother cracks his knuckles, then spits
into the water. Of us two, he's mother's.
I've known always. He has her desire
for something other than's in front of his eyes.
In St. Michael when the company man
told us our tickets were a sham,
they both stood poker-faced, determined.
They didn't need to look at each other
to decide to refuse return passage to Seattle.

Me? Without them, I might have taken it
for a sign, turned back, let fate decide
my course.

The Old Man and I, blue-eyed and rowdy,
don't expect much. We feel
lucky instead of left behind.
Once I watched him get throwed out of a bar,

pull himself up on the lamppost, and dust off his hat,
then, smiling, toddle across the street to another.

Mother has big plans—laundry, hotel,
restaurant—and Tommie will prop her up.
Me, I'll wait, see what happens.
I can brush myself off and walk away.

She called me Gusty as a baby
because I cried so much,
that my eyes were hardly ever open
like I didn't want to see the world
for all the tears she said,

but it wasn't that.
I could see what I'd been born into
and I hadn't gotten yet used to the idea
that the best answer to bad luck
was to brush yourself off and move on.
These days I don't bother with tears.

I watch the bank from the stern, see the cuts and sweepers,
the riffles along the eddy's edge, the changes
the steamer leaves in its wake. My brother,
he looks ahead, where the bow splits
the river into two sides before it passes through.

Nellie Considers Her Sons: Dark

—Standing at the rail of a sternwheeler on the Yukon River, Summer 1898

On the steamer north,
night sloughs away with latitude,
fading at the edge first.
Black sky, then gray,
then twilight steeped in blue.
Then always light.
Morning and evening, twins.
The meal's menu marks
the only difference.

The sun carves its circle
like the long hand on a pocket watch.
Every second has its brother
at the opposite side.

My eyes rest on the boys' faces,
their clear eyes, the hollow of their cheeks.
Brothers, rough copies,
one page imprinted
by the heavy writing
on the first.

Tom already old enough to go his own way
and Elmer nearly, bringing
them North to find their father
is my last act as mother to the boys
they were once. When this trip is over,
they'll be men.

But even in July, already three golden leaves
punctuate the paper birch across the river.
Even in the heat, so stifling today
that I stand at the back of the steamer
and watch the wheel to breathe
the cold the paddles drag up
from under the brown water.
In spite of the light, winter rests
in the darkness at the river's bottom,
gathering its strength before it returns.

On Dominion Creek Tom Makes a Decision

—Dominion Creek, Yukon Territory, Summer 1898

Everything goes into the ground:
my father's money, my labor, my brother's moods.
Nothing comes up but dirt, shovel after shovel,
run through the rocker, the sluice.

Dirty laundry's where the money is. Mother rakes it in
pressing and mending, while Elmer and
the Old Man and I, shivering,
lean on the shovel's handle, scratch the grime
on our foreheads and puzzle at the hole
full of nothing.

There isn't dust enough to make me dig deeper.

At the scales in town, men empty their bags,
every grain a world of labor, but there's more money
to wring it out of their pants in the laundry or dance hall.

The old man should drink the water running out of the sluice
instead of letting the barkeep skim off a share.
He'd get as much nothing from water
as he gets on this claim.

The wheelbarrow's hardened his back into a question mark.
His clawed hand tries to answer with a scratch,
an evening rub of liniment, the stench
soaks into his bed.

Mother staked on promises.
For all the promise, he earns only
dollars a day, while the dry hole
he owns stays buried under curses and sweat.

While Mother, steam burns and sweat,
hands as raw as a plucked hen,
knots her full purse. Even poor, men need washing,
and the rich, they have no time to sew.
The Old Man digs and stinks
while she makes the living.
I may have no wringer, no sewing machine,
but I have the sense to drop this pickaxe
and head back into town.

Nellie Considers Her Sons Again: Light

—Dawson City, Yukon Territory, December 1899

As the daylight faded, I let go.
Small things at first:
a thimble lost to the foxtail in front of the cabin,
the writing paper swamped in the river.
Then, recipes abandoned for lack of butter.
Finally, that promise that being together would mean
the pleasure of leaving something behind.

Even the snow is blackened
with wood smoke. The gray twilight we call
morning visits at noon and then darts away.

My boys buried in wool blankets
in the corner of the cabin,
stir in their sleep, bothered
by the scratch of my pen.

In this way they have always been alike:
stern eyes, slow to smile,
steeped in gravity.

Grown, they put dinner on our table,
caribou and duck. They feed me.

Winter days stay only a little while,
indifferent, sleepy,
like my baby, the boy so long gone
I squint to see him

in the man who follows
his father to the dance hall
and stumbles home late.

His brother looks after
him, takes him to the woods,
away from this dark town,
from his wild self, the half
he didn't get
from me.

But even with Tom's keeping,
he'll wander and I'll wonder how
to make myself certain
of his survival.

Races on the Fourth of July

—Dawson City, Yukon Territory, 1900

They line the street five deep.

Roofs, clear of snow, capped
on this hot day with men,
legs dangling like icicles.

A few women in the balconies
above the surveyor's office,
rapt, lean toward

two horses,
two riders,

one dusty blur.

Everyone wants to know:
who's first?

Even in sun,
the answer
chills,

like the second
before anyone else knows
what you found in the gravel.

Who's first?
is the only question
that matters here.

RACES ON FOURTH OF JULY IN DAWSON, 1900. DARMS PHOTO.

Lost Luxury

—Dawson City, Yukon Territory, 1900

I didn't blink at the man,
his chained black bear
its leather dog collar
denting the dark fur.

He fed it scraps
from his left hand
while its nose nuzzled his palm.

Nuzzled, not long ago
I would have said that about my babies.

I might have looked back,
noted the thick links of chain,
the scraps cupped in his palm,

been surprised
by the man's ease,
his bent leg, slouched back,
the bear's calm, doglike posture,
the comfort they brought each other.

But here the sun spins around
the summer sky, and in winter
lights twist through
the dark. Surprise
is a luxury beyond my means.

Correspondence: Free Miner's Certificate

—Dawson City, Yukon Territory, August 28, 1900

DATE OF ISSUE_____

No. 74309

DOMINION OF CANADA

FREE MINER'S CERTIFICATE.

PLACE OF ISSUE_____ NON-TRANSFERABLE. VALID FOR ONE YEAR ONLY.

This is to Certify that *J. H. Gibson*

of_____ *has paid me this day the*

sum of *ten dollars* *and is entitled to all the rights and*

privileges of a Free Miner, under any Mining Regulations of the Government

of Canada, for one year from the twenty-eighth day of August A.D. 1900.

This Certificate shall also grant to the holder thereof the privilege of Fishing and Shooting, subject to the provisions of any Act which has been passed, or which may hereafter be passed for the protection of game and fish; also the privilege of Cutting Timber for actual necessities, for building houses, boats, and for general mining operations; such timber, however, to be for the exclusive use of the miner himself, but such permission shall not extend to timber which may have been heretofore or which may hereafter be granted to other persons or corporations.

Countersigned,

J. E. Bolduc

To be Countersigned by the Gold Commissioner,
Mining Recorder, or by an Officer or
Agent of the Department of Interior.

Deputy of the Minister of the Interior.

Tom Breaks Cargo on the Steamers

—Dawson City, Yukon Territory, 1901

No matter how little goes out, something comes in.
Someone has to break cargo. I heft pianos,
carry rolls of silk, and grunt
case after case of whiskey,

so the steamer's mouth can yawn
open for the next load of men.
They sell everything they dragged
over the Pass to afford their passage back.

At least they load themselves
as I watch from the dock.
Then, I wait, one steamer unloaded,
one downriver churning its way here.

Nothing to tote for a while, I could lie
down in the sun; I could go for a drink,
but either would leave me too soft for work,
so instead I paddle upriver

to the good duck spot,
birds so thick on the water, you'd think
the river was feathered. From there, I can hear
the steamer's blast upriver and paddle,

with the current's care, to make it back
to break on dock and make a few dollars,
a side dish to a quarry of birds.
Some afternoons, I abandon a just flushed covey

and hurry to beat the freighter to its moorage.
In that race, kneeling in the center of the canoe,
paddle flashing one side to the other
trailing silver beads, with the patterned

slosh and pull of the effort, I forget
the fever for gold that has swallowed
this town whole. My shotgun leans against

the thwart and I wish that all my life
could be this breeze, this pull toward a blast,
this hurry, rather than the slow gasps
and chocks of the pickaxe and the grind
of the wheelbarrow on uneven trails.

I wish for a life that I work for
rather than one that makes work of me.
This winter, when both the steamers
and I sit idle for lack of open water,

Mother will set the table
behind the piles of laundry,
and we'll feast on roast duck or grouse stew.
We'll feast on the good work I made

of the summer between unloading
crates full of work
other men made
for themselves.

Letter from Home

—Windham, Ontario, October 1901

Dear Nellie,

You say you are dressmaking.
I can see the ribs and thread,
feel needles through the thick
of your thumb.

I remember your delicate stitches.
My fingers trace the hem in this blue silk
and I can see you
biting your lip and squinting
over the needle's tip.

You spoke of photographs, but if you sent
them I never got them.

Which women have the money
to buy dresses there?

Mother, always anxious,
wrings her handkerchief,
pulls the threads,
and longs.

She sets a place
at the table for Worry,
who sweeps her black skirt aside
while she smoothes the napkin
on her lap. I hear
Mother whispering to her
evenings in front of the fire.

Tell the boys to dig hard
and get rich and come away
from that awful country.

Your loving sister,

Mary Jane

Joe, at the Dance Hall

—Dawson City, Yukon Territory, 1902

Nellie's faith, her sacrifice, lies in water.
She suffers scalding and the line the metal
washtub scars into her palm with grace. My life is the shovel
heaved for another man; my word
my every promise comes to nothing but mud.
She expects too much. It's her fault I raise this glass.

It's her fault my hand plants this glass
on the bar. My wife, waterlogged
with laundry and virtue, scrubs money from the mud,
and in doing so, washes me away, my true mettle.
Four years ago I gave her my word.
Tonight, against it, I raise a shovel,

throw mud after promises, and shovel
out dust from my pockets to pay for this glass.
I don't know if there is a word
for a man like me. If there is, it sounds like water
riffling through the sluice, meddling
with the marriage I've turned into mud.

In four years so much work, so much mud.
There, the cabin, Nellie's business. Here, whores shove
against me and their lips taste like metal.
Mine, like dirt. In the saloon the only clean glass
is the mirror that shows our reverse, as silver as water.
My future glares as dim and worn as the carved word

worked into the bar, an angry word
scratched by another drunk with mud
under his fingers, who heard only the whisper of water,
the creek above or below discovery, a promise, until the shovel
unbuttoned his soul, passed him the shot glass,
ran her fingernails across the top of his belt, meddling

with his intentions. I longed to prove different, but there is no medal
for husbandry. I came seeking color. Some men have it lucky, no word
sent home, none returned, no wife, no glass
in which to see themselves. My home, muddied
with her syllables, my hand, raw with shoveling,
raises with her volume. At morning, I see myself in creek water,

as I scratch for more metal, breaking my back over mud.
I have no word to give anymore, and as I shovel
I think of raising the glass, not of the eyes staring back from the water.

Montana Steam Laundry

—Dawson City, Yukon Territory, September 1902

After the sluice box all day, the men resent the water,
lay blame to it, their hands caked in dirt.
I watch them, open the door, read the gray
hunger of their skin. Where men prospect, women wash
the harsh life out of the land, out of men, wring
what's left of their souls from the rough

landscape. My hands are still slender, skin rough,
reddened from soap, boiling water.
Here, everyone struggles. I wring
our living out of this frozen dirt,
ache, over this old tub. My husband washes
it all down in the saloon. Either the gray

flask in his coat or the shot glass, speckled gray
grime on the bar. He drinks. I take in wash.
I knew this marriage was too rough
to be smoothed by time and creek water.
I walk. Pick smooth stones, rub off the dirt,
line them up on the windowsill. I want to wring

some meaning out of this life. Instead I wring
woolen socks, drawers, shirts gray
with labor. The Klondike, my dirty
chance to save my boys the roughness
of a poorer life. I wanted a baptism, water
poured over foreheads, to wash

them of pain and fear, wash
myself too. Instead, reeking, he wrings
my neck in their sight. The river's water
flows west toward the new camp, the gray
light of hope. A woman alone has it rough.
Some dance, some sing, some dirty

themselves with men, so many, so much dirt,
but I will be well-off someday, washed
away in the tide of money this rough
land promises. At the handle, my hands wring
out another man's clothes. Gray
suds darken the cooling water.

My boys are rough. They can make pay dirt.
New camp, new water. My hands washed
of him, this gold ring gone before spring's gray light.

Will Butler Waits outside the Laundry

—Dawson City, Yukon Territory, March 1903

Men do things for women:
open doors, carry packages, shave.
Most times, we don't mean it.

Today, lurking outside the laundry,
waiting for Hannah Mullen to leave,
I mean it. If I wait, Mrs. Gibson

will take my laundry, pass me a receipt
while I pass the time, noticing her fingers
playing with the pen, noticing

the way she folds bills before
tucking them away. I've paid
her some attention, observed

long eyelashes, a hand fluttering
to smooth hair at my entrance,
the smile that rises higher on the left.

I have never been a man
to steal, but her marriage seems
more a suggestion

than a contract. Gibson is never here,
so I wait for the hired help to leave,
that I might talk alone a few minutes

with her. At the dance hall,
it would be easy, a little dust and a little time,
but I lurk here instead, shamed

to admit the buzz of spring in my joints.
The sun sets less each night
and I feel it at my shoulder.

In March, mornings, ice crackles over
the puddles, and by supper it's melted
to mud. A movement

from solid to liquid, repeated
daily as I melt into a younger self.
I think she does too.

I fidget, waiting,
like every shoot buried
under the snow.

A slam and a step, and Hannah's out.
She pulls on gloves. I nod, tip
my hat, and shift the bundle

of my laundry to my other arm
to open the door.

Hannah Mullen

—Dawson City, Yukon Territory, March 30, 1903

When I was little, people would exclaim over my red hair
Oh, a pretty girl, such curls, while my sister
seethed at my side, brown-headed and wrong.
I smiled, swallowing praise like water.

I grew on it into something finer,
a teacup, gold paint and flowers.
Something thin, lashy, and wanting
attention, and more than that, money.

I thought the Klondike would be my making.
A petticoat, some garters, and the dust would roll in.
I thought my red hair would help. I bounced
curls on my shoulders, practiced glances,

and believed the stage hall would
offer me something more than this old dress,
laundry-water damp at the hem.
At least, these days, I go home smelling of soap.

I used to go home smelling of off-key piano
strings and cigars. I would go to sleep still feeling
fingers digging into my skin. Sometimes, if it was late
enough and I was drunk enough, I would fall asleep

while some miner rocked the bed springs through me.
I used to dream of running downhill
breathless toward a river where a boat full to the rails
steamed away without me.

Then, I'd wake on the cot in my crib to the sound
of breaking glass. When Nellie caught me crying
behind the laundry, bloody and blackened, she thought
she could prove her goodness through my saving.

She thought there was nothing needles and ribbons
couldn't fix, and when she heard I had a little
saved myself, she saw her chance in my purse.
There are women who make money other ways.

We could be them she said, so I work
for her for a while until we gather
the cash to set out without her husband
for the new camp in all the headlines.

She wants a hotel, boarders, a bar,
and I said yes, I'd help with washing to get
to work in the daylight again. Not that this town
even has that all the time, but to work in something

that I can say I do, to write home a word or two
of truth. Some jobs have names, while others catch
in the back of the throat, turn your eyes down
before you can get them out. I had forgotten

the taste of honest words, salty-sweet on the tongue.
I thought I'd always have red curls and sweet lips,
but the dance hall taught me that a little while
is the only while there is, and the flashes of sense

in the din are all we get. So now it's her and Will
and me, a partnership drawn at the attorney's.
I hope in this new camp I will be everything
I hadn't been here. But I have doubts.

Maybe if I hadn't started here. Maybe if I hadn't
had curls. Maybe if I hadn't told her
about the money. If she hadn't
taken me in, I'd be certain at least of the path

to my own end. For the first time in a long time
I want something. If it means hanging on with them,
then that's what I mean to do.

Correspondence: A Contract, Witnessed, Sealed, and Signed

—Dawson City, Yukon Territory, April 2, 1903

ARTICLES OF AGREEMENT, made and entered into the second day of April, A. D. 1903, at Dawson, Yukon Territory, Canada, BETWEEN William Butler, of the first part, Hannah Mullen, of the second part, and Sarah Ellen Gibson, of the third part, all temporarily residing at Dawson, aforesaid;

WHEREAS, the said parties here to intend to leave the Yukon Territory and go to the District of Alaska for the purpose of entering into the business of conducting a roadhouse and also intend to engage in the purchasing and selling of supplies, goods, wares, and merchandise;

AND, WHEREAS, the said parties severally own provisions and supplies necessary for their journey and the conduct of said road-house business;

NOW, THEREFORE, THESE PRESENTS WITNESSETH: That the said parties hereto have agreed, and by these present do agree, to become copartners together in the business aforesaid, and all things thereto appertaining, as well as in the provisions and supplies now severally owned by them, as aforesaid, to be used in the conduct of said business, as aforesaid, and which they severally contribute as the joint assets of said business; which said partnership it is agreed, shall continue from the date of these presents until either of the parties hereto shall notify the other in writing of his or her or their intention to dissolve the same, upon thirty days' notice, at the expiration of which time the said copartnership shall be considered dissolved and an account and settlement of the partnership affairs be had and taken.

And also that they shall and will, during the life of said copartnership, discharge equally among them all expenses incurred in the conduct of said business;

And that all such profit, gain, and increase as shall arise by reason of said business shall be equally and proportionately divided among them, share and share alike. And also all losses that shall or may happen in the said business, by bad debts, bad commodities, or otherwise, shall be paid and borne equally among them.

That the said parties hereto further agree, that in case of the death of either of them, the surviving parties shall make a true and final account of all business transactions of said copartnership to the heirs, executors, or administrators of the party deceased, and in all things well and truly adjust the same; and also, that upon making such account, all and every asset, as well as the gain and increase thereof, which shall appear to the remaining, shall be equally parted and divided among them, the said copartners, their heirs, executors or administrators, share and share alike.

IN WITNESS THEREOF, the said parties to these presents have hereunto set their hands and seals, the day and year first written above.

Will Packs His Fiddle and Sings

—Dawson City, Yukon Territory, April 1903

Love like the bow loves the string,
like the high whine of the fiddle
muffled through the dance hall's wall
catches your ear on the street.

Love like piano keys itch for touch
while the empty arc of fingers
whispers to the air over ivory.

Love the way the notes love the emptiness
the second before music rises,
the way the banjo loves the voice
with a bum ditty.

Love the way that worn gold latch
of the musician's case snaps an end
on an evening so late
it has turned to morning.

If that snap shut is the beginning,
then let the fiddle be the last thing I pack.

If departure is both opening
and closing, then let it
clatter just a little
before the fiddle, longing
in its red velvet bed,
starts its wait.

Nellie Thinks She Should Have Waited for the Boat

—On the trail, Dawson to Fairbanks, May 1903

Tanana Station, fifty men, not one
woman. We are the only two white women

ever came here and still I am alone.
She is no good at all. Travel without

a woman seemed foolish, more foolish than
leaving the boys and their father, ever

drunk. Gold camp is harder for a woman than
a man. For them, a home warms with us—fire

our cooking, kindling our skirts. For us home
calls in letters from sisters—a rough broom

fashioned from dry birch twigs. A worn wringer
steamed upriver is our sluice, our pay dirt.

We know only two ways to mine miners.
I was a fool to bring her from Dawson.

He told me I would find Hannah out before
I reached here, but I thought of work, the tubs,

steam burning our hands back at the laundry.
I thought another woman would help, feared

loneliness among men, their cussing, spit.
Ice, not steam, is the test of a woman.

The whores know: their cold art, picking pockets
I patched. On this trail the ice destroyed her.

Some days she would be all right, the next, not speak.
What was wrong no one could tell. Her silence

muffled in her coat, her eyes empty, blue
as the sky above the ridgeline. I drove

the brown horse and the load into here. Will
drove the gray. Bill drove the dogs. Me,

drawing over tussocks with that narrow
sleigh and a top-heavy load. I never

asked myself to do anything this hard,
not leaving my husband, or my boys, back

at the cabin. Some nights I was clear
to the waist, upsetting on snow, flowing

around in it to get straight again. When
I harnessed him, one of the horses hit

me in the mouth, broke my front tooth in half.
I have the other half in my pocket.

Some nights my clothes froze around me, circles
of icy skirt, soggy wool, black boots cracked.

Will would tell her to get me something warm
and she would answer that she was as wet.

I want to pay her her share. She can't work
for me no more. We will let her out. Free

ourselves from the weight of her investment.
We've enough to lug there, the grub, the sleighs,

Will, his broken past, my broken marriage,
soon the boys too. I'll send for them. They can

hunt. They'll build cabins, stake claims, be more help
than her. Buying out her share, she can't say

that either of us cheated her. I have
stayed honest so far. I wish I had waited

for the boat, wish there was profit in truth,
but in a new camp land goes, pockets fill fast,

staking first is the business. On this trip
my regrets left tracks while my feet skated

on the overflow, leaving a shadow,
but it is all over now, the hardness

of life. There is not another woman
could or would do all I have done, or would

have driven a horse on the road I did.

Tom Makes a Narrow Escape

—Just upriver from Dawson, May 29, 1903

Two miles upriver this morning
the canoe turned turtle and I found
myself caught under the boat
because Jesse and I fired from the same side.
Our blast turned us both over and into the Yukon.

I had called and the flock passed over our heads
as we blazed away. Jesse lost his gun,
but I clung to mine,

and as I came up, my head shattered the surface.
Jesse, always the swimmer, had climbed on top of the canoe.
I grabbed on and it sank again.
And like a comedy, for minutes
as one of us got hold the other pulled away.
There went the canoe sinking and tipping,
over and over with each of us struggling for breath.
It rolled and I went under, and before
I could come up again, I let the gun go.
My hip boot, filled with water, fought
to pull me under.
We grabbed and rolled that damn canoe
a third time before we got the sense
to grab at different ends and balance each other out.

In the current, soaked and cold,
clutching the upended gunwales,
we drifted past McDonald Island
where Hatch, the old farmer, heard us calling out.

He paddled out and pulled us ashore.
It was fifteen minutes before either of us
had breath enough to tell him what happened.

When finally our words poured out
onto the pebbled bank,
they shattered and glistened.
Jesse babbled and I interrupted,
tangled in the threads of our own panic.

But Hatch, thin-lipped, said nothing,
but shook his head slow
and looked at his shoes.

It was a hard row back,
empty-handed, in a canoe
with borrowed paddles,
a hard row, to bring ourselves back
into Dawson that night.

Tom and Elmer Dive for the Gun

—Just upriver from Dawson, May 30, 1903

Elmer, some things a man can ask only of a brother.
Diving headlong into the Yukon is one,
but that gun cost me so much, I had to ask.
Fifty-five dollars and it fed us

and half of Dawson all winter.
So we each took turns in the water.
Our ration, a big swallow of air
before each blind grapple for the bottom.

I hoped I could catch something,
graze the edge of the barrel
knock into the chunk of stock,
but I knew that even feeling it,

my breath might give out before my grip.
When I came up to drink some air,
you were wrapped in a wool blanket,
looking plate-eyed into the water.

As I heaved myself over the gunwale,
you said, *That was long, I wasn't sure you were coming up,*
in a tone drier than we had been all morning.
Even on that warm day,

we shivered. The night before I couldn't sleep
for hope that my losses wouldn't be so final.
Without saying so, you told me to stop.
The gun was gone.

Even if I drowned for trying, the river had it.
We picked up the paddles, and with the current's
grace, dipped and pulled our tired selves back toward home.

Not Near as Wild

—Dawson City, Yukon Territory, June 6, 1903

Dear Mother,

We are the same since you left.
Elmer is decking
on the *LaFrance* and has gone
on his second trip already.
He gets $75 a month clear.
He's trying; I'll give him that.

But he buys cigars and tobacco.
He has been pretty straight so far, not near as wild
as last winter. I am getting him broke off it,
but it takes following him evenings
when he's in town and keeping him in most nights.
Fisher, the duck kid, is with him as mess boy
and he teases him to death
that I'm like a wife,
swinging a broomstick
in the dance hall, but Gusty takes it
in stride, like everything. His blue eyes
smirking under his cap.

Since you wondered, the Old Man
stayed here in the cabin for a few weeks when
Boyle came after him to work
running his sawmill plant
at the mouth of Bear Creek.
I had a hell of a time to get him to take it.
He wanted a job in town

so he could live off the kid and me.
Every time Boyle came up the porch,
the Old Man climbed out the back
bedroom window and ran off.
If he could have been paid for the work
he put into avoiding work, me and Gusty
could have lived off of him.
Him and I had a few stormy interviews,
but he went. Then, he would make
every excuse to get back to town,

so we had another interview,
involving a broken chair
and overturned table, but he got the point.
He is at work now, but near a roadhouse,
so he won't have much coming.
I won't let the Old Man quit.

Between the two of them, I'm a handler.
One night Gusty sings
as I wrestle him out of the saloon.
The next night Old Man, swings
fists wildly and falls off the stool
as I drag him toward the door.

Maybe I understand a little
what it was like for you in the cabin.
In the winter the lamp's flicker
and pen's scratch keeping you company,
and in the summer the arc of the sun
on the wall all night.

Minding people who don't care to be minded
isn't the work I'm used to,
but it's what I've drawn for now.

Your loving son,

Tom Gibson

Elmer Considers the Old Man Drinking

—Dawson City, Yukon Territory, August 1903

Watching him drink quart
after quart of beer,
four in the space
of our conversation,
I notice my own knuckles
rounding the glass.

I'm sent to tell him
there's a letter waiting.
He tells me he hopes
for a black border,
an envelope brooding with news
of a death back home.
He pins his hopes on money,
maybe a house.

I've watched him stagger
and strike, swagger
and shatter. How many
sons look for their father
in the dance hall and find
him in the back room,
puzzling over the buttons
on a whore's dress while she
waits for him to pass out?

How many sons still raise
the glass to their lips and drink?

When he turns on the stool,
the legs creak a weak protest.
His arm, meant
to rest on my shoulder
nearly knocks me from my chair.
He mutters, *What's coming*
to me, son. What's coming.
Not a question, a declaration.
As if he just waits long enough
on this bar stool,
he'll get somewhere.

The New Camp

—Fairbanks, Alaska, December 1903

Some towns glitter
in the blue of a January
morning, snow as clean
as souls on Sunday
afternoon.

Some sleep in, lazing
in the moist heat,
warring against all motion
while they listen to the water
swallowing the sand.

In others, hoarse voices calling out
and the shuffling of thousands of feet
mark the beginning of another busy day.

Here, fog curtains the windows,
so thick this morning,
that as I huff and slide
down the icy street,
no one inhabits the dull glow
of the windowpanes.

At one cabin I see a handprint,
melted into the ice inside
the glass. Five fingers
tear the frost's gray cloth.

Through them, I glimpse
lamplight and motion,
just before the cold rushes
to rebuild its gray cocoon.

Steam

—Fairbanks, Alaska, January 1904

In the teapot's black
spout, steam whispers,
gurgles, then streams.

Steam, like spring fog
on the low
lake at dawn,
yawns out of
the washtub's mouth.

In the stewpot,
chunks of moose, an onion
with the rot peeled away, the last
of the summer's potatoes
bubble, and steam
soaks the lifted lid,
a perfect moon, dripping
round and hopeful.

The smell of steam
sweetened with honey
rises out of
the teacup, a daffodil
open on the dark tabletop.

Lips rounded,
I defeat it with my breath,
and steam flees
with the wave
of my hand.

Is it joy—lingering above
the surface, hastening
away?

Infidelity

—Fairbanks, Alaska, January 1904

If he looks sidelong
as the door swings open,
pretend not to notice.

If he asks you,
smile and look through your lashes
at the scar just above his left eye.

Take in that curve, the tender-looking skin,
but remember how rough it feels to the touch.

If you find words
have escaped you,
like the ice that cracks

along the banks of the river in spring
when frozen boulders
tear through the bridge,

don't forget; people line
the banks then, hungry
for slices of daylight and wind.

They listen to the ice grind
and the high-pitched whine
of wood posts about to give way.

If you hear the clamor of a crowd,
know they applaud destruction.

Know that spring is the same
as what you have done.

The difference is in the number of eyes
and the wood smoke of hushed conversation
rising out of the cabins at night.

Once you tear out the pilings,
you make your own way
across the river,

while they draw plans
for the new summer's bridge.

Tom Returns to Dawson

—Dawson City, Yukon Territory, June 14, 1904

Dear Mother,

You will have to excuse this writing
as the table is rough and the pencil
runs away with itself.

I expected a letter on the last steamer,
but she is in and I have not got it yet.
Judging from your last telegram, there will be no letter.
If you want to know how it is in Dawson these days,
you could ask. But you don't. I'd tell you it is dying,
the river steals the people as town wastes away.

Every letter I get from you is a shopping list.
No news, no greetings, no thanks.
Just sugar, hatpins, whiskey, cigars,
fabric, and the boiler.
Too many pounds for me to freight.
Do you think I have got an airship or rolled a bank?
It takes a little money to get to the mouth of the river from here.
Or don't you remember.
At the new camp, it's dreams and aspirations,
but here I can barely make enough to make it home myself.
The bank has taken your cabins for want of mortgage and renters.
You knew when you sent me I was going
to have to make enough to take me back,
but there's no breaking down boats because nothing comes in.
Everyone's packing to leave.

You must see them all getting off the steamers
on the Chena, breaking half of Dawson on the docks.
You couldn't give a real gold brick away
at any price here now.

If you want to know how I am,
it takes two to three dollars to keep me and the dogs here.
Lady had a dozen and I drowned eight.
Sally had five and I killed two.
None of them had their eyes open yet.

I took them from Lady and bagged them, squirming,
in a flour sack with some rocks.
Before I threw it into the river,
I felt the tremble of breath under burlap
and thought of the strong ones and what they'd pull next winter
when I hunt meat for the new camp.

I won't be back here and that suits me fine.

Don't wait or worry about me. I will come
as soon as I get enough to start.

Your son,

Tom

Elmer is
cutting top off
trees so winds
won't blow down this
cache 33 head

Luck Conspires against Tom and Elmer

—Twelve Mile Summit, 85 miles outside of Fairbanks, Alaska

October 31, 1904

The caribou have finished, been through here and we missed them.
All that work only to bag six stragglers.

We wait, decide to move downhill,
where the snow isn't as deep,

and watch for another herd to make its run. This cold,
we'll have to build a line cabin. I hand Elmer the axe.

I haul, Elmer chops, chipping wells into logs for other logs.
I can hear the temperature dropping, a crackling in the air,

a deepening thud from my boots. It numbs
my face, pricks my lungs, making in-breaths heavy.

I listen to my breath, a two-stroke pull and push.
I hear my effort, and, then, a cry, *God Damn.*

I look up to see Elmer's boot split open, red spread on the snow.
His right foot, a bloody mess, and his hands quaking around the axe handle.

Another *God Damn, Shit.* I think first of the cold,
the logs stacked and waiting to be hewn and restacked,

our survival, then I think of our mother, her fretting telling me,
Keep your eye on your brother, how when I was young she'd whisper

Hold Gusty's hand near the street, and how on the steamer I was to keep him
away from the older boys. God Damn. Even, both of us men,

he's the kid. Even, both of us men, he's careless with an axe.
Two toes almost gone, he crouches, pushing his cloven boot together,

as if will could fuse it, undo a moment's inattention.
I pull off my mitts, tuck them into my armpit and bend to look at his foot.

When I pull at the split boot, he winces.
I prop him against the sled, pile blankets under his leg, start a fire

and set to work with the axe. Without shelter we'll both go down,
with one axe the shelter will take longer. The arc of the weighted axe head,

the dull thud saves me by degrees. Swing and thud, swing and thud.
I don't hear the prospector until he is upon me with a *Hallo,*

in need of help? If he hadn't, on his long hike into town, seen
the campfire and stopped to help with the axe, I'd hate to think,

but then, mostly, about all this, I hate to think.

November 2, 1904

After the cabin is built, everything snugged away, the prospector gone,
leaving Elmer wrapped and propped, I mush to Circle,

but there, everyone starving out the cold, all they can
give me is whiskey and medicine, no food.

I take that to Elmer and go on for another thirty-five miles to Miller Creek for flour,
maybe sugar, and a little coffee. If we have to wait out healing in the shack

we'll need something besides six caribou. Some people on the way to Fairbanks,
having missed the herd too, trade flour for meat. And I think of luck

and accidents, the way those six stragglers damn near saved our lives,
the way the sourdough showed up and with food and an axe.

Just as I think luck is for once turning for my good, I fall,
wrenching my knee around. It's all I can do to stand, let alone walk.

The dogs don't stop, and I have to whistle and shout, limp along
yelling behind them. Until finally Moose realizes my weight

has unburdened the sled and stops. The trail's too narrow for the team
to turn, so he waits me out, while I bumble along, muttering,

but grateful for that dog, for raising him from a puppy,
for him having enough sense to make the team stop,

and for them with sense enough to follow him. I ball my hands into fists,
to keep off the pain of straightening my knee.

On the sled, again I stand on one leg, lean on my hip,
and let the dogs drag me back to the cabin.

God Damn, I tell Elmer, *If we survive this, we'll be fine sourdoughs.*
He replies, *If we survive this, I'll be surprised and we'll be broke.*

The truth in that smarts. It's not just his toes, but our livelihood.
All our cash sunk on this trip, we missed the caribou.

I wonder at what we're going to lose. Shake my head.
He mutters, *What doesn't kill you only tries harder the next time.*

November 5, 1904

We were a party of two, but our disappointment has become a
third man, leaning against the rickety wall of this shack.

He pushes his feet close to the fire and crosses his arms
while I watch the cloud of his breath, see his hands stuck into

his armpits for warmth. His hat's pulled down over his eyes
as he rocks his back against the logs to get comfortable.

I stew in regret, worry on money, worry on mother.
Elmer can't think for pain, and we lie,

wrapped against frost and shivering, all night. When the lights
whisper across the sky, a fluid roll, Elmer says he can hear them

popping, sizzling. I watch, wishful for sound,
but I hear nothing but disappointment grunting in his sleep.

November 7, 1904

In the cold clear of the dark morning I heard the click
of caribou knees, like twigs snapping in chorus, the ligaments popping

with each step. Too sore to walk myself, right knee swollen straight,
I peep out the propped logs and watch.

I think of the rifle leaning near the frame, but I know
I can't get a bead on, and even if luck would grace me with

a shot, I won't be able, one-legged, to stand, to gut it, clean it, or
drag it here. And Elmer is even less able than me.

We're two men with two good legs between us holed up in a shack
while the whole herd passes through.

November 10, 1904

We don't speak much, just sit. I think of the moment, just before
I fell, the moment when I still had a chance.

I would plant my feet more firmly on the runners,
turn my shoulder a hair to the left, keep my foot out of the way.

It's the moment in the arc of the swing when opportunity
slices through the air, cleaving the world into before and after,

only the shave of regret in between. We can both walk now,
if you'd call the stumbling we do walking. I can bend my knee,

but don't want to much, and Elmer can get on around
on one foot using cussing as a crutch.

I've done a passing good job on his boot, scraps of harness and rope.
A few more days and we're into town, with Elmer as cargo,

to plot what I'll have to cast off for cash to make it to spring.
Not the cabins, but anything not sitting on the ground will have to go

to fund another hunt, to pull in some cash.
The mule will have to go for less than I paid, and I'll still have to borrow

a little to get by. I won't sell the horses and dog,
but if we can walk, and we can get sheep and mutton, that will fetch

a price back in town. While we lie in, waiting out healing, I've had time
to go over lists in my mind: snowshoes, sighted rifles, wool dungarees,

German socks, parka, tent, Yukon stove, and food. If the sleds can be light
we'll load them all the more and drag them in full.

Sheep meat sells, always sells, and if we can make it
to the hills in November, we'll make good again.

59 - 804 - 150

Correspondence: Handwritten Receipt

—Fairbanks, Alaska, December 9, 1904

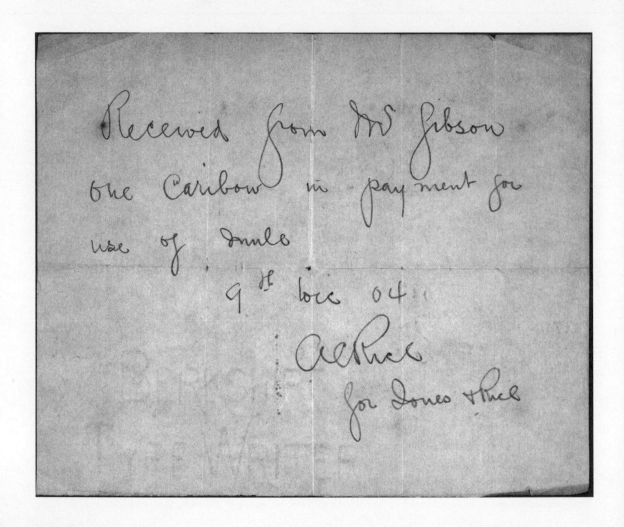

Mother-in-law

—Fairbanks, Alaska, May 1905

Maybe it was my skirt, like yours,
or my hair, curls tangled
with youth.

Maybe it was the way we both brought
our hands to our lips in surprise, or the girl
in me that you had watched come up as you raised
only sons. Something the same in us
led you to warn me.

Leave him before he kills you,

you whispered a week before the wedding,
brush frozen in my hair, as still
as the pins on the dresser.
Our eyes locked in the mirror.

I gauged your tone, the stillness
of your fingers on the back
of my neck, the set of your lips

and turned my eyes down to the mirror's handle,
silver, black patina broken by prints.

His father . . .

you started, moving the brush again,
stroke and pull.

His father,

you repeated, breath weary
with the storm that threatened
every night until his liquid disappearance
shamed and freed you.

I know,

I said and thought of your boy, gray eyes,
his smooth promise, our planned escape

I weighed the mason jar,
its cool contents, the burn in the back of the throat,
my youth, the boy in him, the man not yet born,
and I stayed.

Mother-in-law, I took you at your word,
but it took me twenty-one years to do it in.

I know now what you knew,
my own boys newly men.

In one I see the promise
liquor and time washed away.
In the other I see their father, your son.
I would warn a woman against him,
my own boy, tell her to leave.

Our skirts would rustle, my hand
would freeze on the worn handle of the hairbrush.

She would meet my eyes,
gauge them, and then she would look away.

And I would smooth her hair,
pin it up, and ready her for dinner.

Ellen Welcomes Three Guests: Postage, Medicine, Liquor

—Fairbanks, Alaska, October 1905

Three tenants occupy the table:
my stamps, our bottle of aspirin,
and Will's bottle of whiskey,
gleaming in a rectangle of sun.

The sunlight bows
to the gravity of their chatter,
eavesdropping.

In the cabin's darkest corner
the bed waits, quilt smoothed,
slats quiet of creaks.

Postage, medicine, liquor,
what could they say?

This morning they watched me
stuff the woodstove with too wet
wood, leave the door open,
breathe life back into night's faded fire.

All night they listened to our breathing.

They dole out scraps of comfort
poured into the wide mouth
of the morning's longing.

Hope, a faded map, crumpled
in my hands, guided me to this cabin,
this new bed, built from the spruce
off the cleared lot, its four posts still rough with bark.

Now, remedy is my guest,
borrowing the table. Stamps,
lonely for envelopes, want for my
words. The aspirin wishes to soothe,
and whiskey to silence,
hush the discomfort of a life,
though new, still wanting.

My son asks,
*Did you think you could leave everything
on a riverbank and just drift away?*

No. I packed it myself,
built this house,
chinked logs, made curtains.
I chose what to abandon
and what to drag along.

The half-empty whiskey,
recites, only quieter,
the same story my old husband,
miles away shouted
in a street muddy with spring.

I hear the river, a lull
under the murmured quarrel
of this camp.

The story followed me
like the ache
that chases hard labor,
stiff joints,
soreness, expected,
but not welcome.

Alone in the cabin,
I admire the sunlight,
long to follow its example,

to eavesdrop and pay
attention to the small
gifts waiting on the table,
not wanting for anything more.

Raven

—Fairbanks, Alaska, November 1905

I want to ask you what it is like
to stand solid against the snow,

to swallow the short daylight,
and preen yourself into night.

Woodstove black. Feathers, feet, eyes,
the curve of your beak: one mind.

I move beneath you weighted by
my borrowed skin—

wool skirt, gray ruff, blue coat,
leggings, thick knit hat.

Hauling firewood, I hear your call,
wordless, unfrozen, between the trees;

then, the dry slice of flight
above my head before you disappear.

I see your belly, your wings, their cloak
of certainty, your unified purpose,

and I want to ask you how to survive
winter along this frozen river,

but I only muster the hollow chock
of log on log as I stack the sled.

My body, its cobbled mess,
gangly, lacking grace,

sputters, stops, then goes again.
You glow, live coal, living cinder,

fleeing each evening to the dark hills,
the crooked rookery of spruce

where hundreds of black eyes
dream the same smoldering dream.

Correspondence: A Letter
From Madame M. Yale

—New York, New York, March 21, 1906

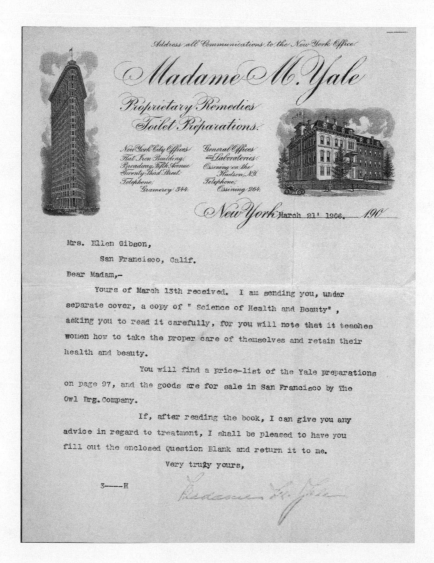

Correspondence: An Unanswered Questionnaire Tucked in a Packet of Letters

—Sent from New York to Fairbanks, Alaska, March 21, 1906

QUESTION BLANK

Kindly answer the following questions and return so that your case may be very carefully studied and proper Yale Remedies recommended. Address all communications to:

MME. M. YALE
Flatiron Building, New York, N. Y.

Married, and How Long?
How Many Children?
How Old Are You?
Does Your Blood Circulate Properly?
Is You Complexion Good or Bad? Describe It.
Are Your Eyes Bright?
Is Your Flesh Firm or Flabby?
What Do You Weigh?
How Tall Are You?
Is the Bust Flat or Well Developed?
Is Your Liver Active?
Are Your Kidneys Active?
Have You Had Any Bladder Trouble?
Is Your Tongue Coated in the Morning?
Is Your Breath Bad at Times?
Does It Hurt You to Walk?
Do You Have Backaches?
Do You Have Any Bearing Down Pains?
Have You a Falling of the Womb?
Is There a Smarting Sensation After Urinating?
How Long Have You Been Sick?

Are You Constipated?
Have You Headaches?
Have You Cold Feet? Do They Get Numb?
Have You Palpitation of the Heart?
Are You Nervous, Irritable, or Impatient?
Do You Suffer Much Pain? If So, Where?
Have You Any Trouble with the Rectum?
Do You Have Pains in the Limbs?
Do Your Feet Swell?
Have You a Good Appetite?
Do You Sleep Well?
Have You Any Stomach Trouble?
Is Your Eyesight Good?
Do You Tremble?
Are You Easily Startled?
Do You Flow Freely or Is the Flow Suppressed?
Do You Suffer Much Pain at the Period Times?
What Is the Color of Your Flow?
Are You Melancholy?
Are You Hysterical?
Do You Worry or Fret About Anything?

Ellen Notices the Dry Spring

—Fairbanks, Alaska, May 1906

If God had a voice,
the wasps
would follow him,

harmonizing.

He made them,
tuned their troubling buzz

himself.

Bees hoard, only
to have us steal
what they've stored;

wasps take only
what's finished.

This dry spring,
they chase me
as I haul out
the slop bucket,

feast on thick water
topped with sludge.

While God, in his gray
paper house,
puts up his feet.

He has no need of
flesh

nor honey.

A Late Answer to Madame M. Yale's Questions

—Fairbanks, Alaska, September 1907

Do I Worry or Fret About Anything?

Yes. Don't you, Madame Yale? Maybe it's paying the rent on your office space,
while I worry about collecting rents, an old lawsuit, and a drawn-out divorce.

We are both women, so where is our connection?
Have you an awful husband? A sweet but drunken lover, too?

I worry about butter, eggs, the dog, Dandy, left
on the chain at his house while I am away.

How can you tell a dog you're afraid you're dying.
One that bites, I mean. No one will take him in.

I'm troubled about Will and Tom fighting over potatoes,
the saw, and land. I'm troubled about potatoes. Yes, them.

Will, too proud over this fall's take, hoards them, lords them over the boys.
Tom, too young and hungry, eats what Will thinks is more than his share.

His share. My share. Will's share. They don't worry about me,
don't know about the pains and changes, don't notice

that I disappear at times behind the curtain that serves as a bedroom,
because the bleeding won't seem to stop.

Will thinks I'm tired, in need of sleep,
but Doctor Sutherland, peeping over my belly,

does not smile. My heels on the bench top,
knees bent, I subject myself to his examination

and stare at the pattern hammered in the tin ceiling of his office,
almost a checkerboard, repeating flowers, anything

to occupy my eyes while his are occupied in me.
Some things I can tell a man, others I cannot, so I settle

for a promise on both sides that they'll share the potatoes
after I'm away.

Correspondence: A Note on a Prescription Pad

—Fairbanks, Alaska, September 1907

For _____ Date _____

R

Thos Gibson Esq.

Your Mother is very seriously ill
with a trouble that is likely to prove
incurable. Have advised her to go
out for treatment as it gives her one
chance for recovery. However the
hopes for her returning are very
slight— Yours Sincerely

J. A. Sutherland, M. D.

Dont tell your Mother this.

Tom Wonders: Is This Sentence for Me or for Her?

—Fairbanks, Alaska, September 1907

Caribou cure
on the rack, hang from bound ankles.
I cut, pull skin from flesh, gut,
and wait. Reread the note from the doctor,
eat a handful of sour cranberries.

Tomorrow, I'll cut roasts,
ribs, and stew meat,
pull the sled into town.
A new sign in the window: fresh meat.
I'll buy whiskey, wait,
pen a letter to my mother.
I have no right to steal hope,
so I'll begin, *Mother, when you recover.*

Melting away, she must know.
I measure my words. The doctor's
sentence determines my slant.

Before I can remember, she held me,
whispering softly. Do I slight
her by leaving out words, leaving in chance?

Tomorrow she leaves. My parting gift, a lie.

September, the last steamers race the ice.
She'll write from the hospital,
tell me she's fine, slight pain

at the incision, fatigue. She'll tell
me to collect her rents, to give
that bastard debtor Condon hell.

In this town, no secret is slight enough
to hide through the winter.
Ice fog whispers, seeps in at corners,
repeats each sentence it overhears.

I still begin, *Mother, when you recover,*
knowing it's a pitted gift,
like the nuggets she'll carry out with her,
something to prove she was once here,
a small burden to carry in her pocket
as she steams away.

Inventory: The Objects in This Hospital Room

—Seattle, Early 1908

A wooden table with clawed feet.

A metal bed with starched yellowed covers.

An empty cobweb in the upper left corner of the window.

The private nurse for fifteen dollars a week.

One empty bottle of beer.

A sister's gloves, folded on the nape of the rocker.

Glass vials and their calcified clinks.

A puddle of gray sunlight on a tiled floor.

Scuffs from visitors' shoes on the left side of the bed.

A photo of Dandy.

The one son able to afford passage.

A hand-carried packet of letters from First Street in Fairbanks.

A dirty glass, half inch of buttermilk in the bottom.

The glass of water, empty,

a pitcher waiting beside it for thirst.

Until Payment Can't Be Made

—Fairbanks, Alaska, January 12, 1908

My Dearest Ellen,

When I learned to write, the teacher praised
my penmanship, the only praise I got
in a school built of switches and paddles.
That pen, its pressure leaving a mark
on my finger, kept me in the desk
for a while, and that while enough,
to make these clear letters
arch in grace despite their sorrow.

Like the rest of First Avenue,
I send this by Tommie to Seattle
in a packet sealed with good-bye.

Once, after falling out with you,
I steamed downriver angry and alone
until regret overtook anger,
and I wrote and told you to come
or else I would come back to you.
You came, but not before I,
missing your letter,
took my passage back to you.

We, steaming in opposite directions,
passed somewhere with the river between us,
not knowing enough to wave.

That seems a story for the papers:
letter-crossed lovers crossing paths,
with a love untempered
by a divorce never granted,
by overprotective sons, by the ruin
of their finances, lawsuits, and age.

Love didn't choose us for ease.
Even our dogs don't get along.
Lady never settled to forgive
Dandy for her ear.

For us, that story ended in finding each other again.
After the long and costly loop
we spun of argument and forgiveness,
we lived at the hotel, separate rooms
borne of our separate names,
so that I had to sneak in the dark hall at night
to come to you and leave at daylight.

Another story for the papers: morning comes too soon
while a man hides behind drapes, pronounces an aubade,
then hastens away. A woman, reaching for her robe,
pats her hair back into order.

Mrs. Natter, puffed up with owning her own hotel,
sympathized until she realized we wouldn't pay her
extra for her sympathy.

She wrote: *Don't think for a moment*
that I was blind for he was seen
coming out of your room in the morning.
Even the cook made remarks,
her angular letters betraying her fury
over the $27.50 we refused to add
to her going rate.

Anything goes until payment can't be made.

This time I have no story for the papers.
A man will not rush to his lover's side,
whisper, hold her hand.

I could not get a dollar. I tried to raise money
for my passage, to sell some of the dogs,
but you will have to make it alone.
I hope that you will have faith in God
and your doctor and make up your mind
that you are going to get well.

But since I don't believe that grace will take a hand in this,
I need to assure you, whatever you say about my share,
don't worry. For I will do anything to please you,
and I promise you that although your sons
and I can't get along together,
for your sake alone, I will not start trouble.

What is yours will be theirs.
What was mine left me when you left.

Don't worry. I will keep Dandy for you,
even though he snaps at me. Someday he'll stop,
and it will be my last loss to know that even he
could forget his fidelities.

I now must close, Ellen, to hunt up Tommie,
give him this to give to you. There will be weeks
between the moment my hand seals this page
and yours responds in opening.

I send my love to you. I hope you
will be pleased to hear from me
even only on this page. I am sorry.

Your Love,

Will Butler

Remembering the River Crossing

—Seattle, Washington, May 1908

In the room you hear the sound of brown river water,
the wake lapping behind the canoe.

You sit in the bow.

Your fingers smooth your skirt, puffed along the gunwale.
You smell the wet dog hunched between your knees,
scratch his ears, and tighten your grip on his collar.
You'll wash his muddy paw prints out of your hem tomorrow.

You hear sounds of the morning, creaking of stove doors, and the ticking of iron
as it heats. You hear the purr of the kettle.

You think *This is the morning* before you remember
there is no morning as long as you keep your eyes shut.

Then you see the canoe overturned against the log wall,
buried in snow, the canoe on the water trailing a wake,
the canoe loaded with moose from upriver.

Then you wonder if the bed is solid.

You never wondered that about the dirt,
the road, the wooden boardwalk.
You crossed the river ice, back and forth all winter,
and never thought of the rushing gurgle
waiting underneath.

You never questioned mud.

There was always a bottom to the river
and the spring was always soggy,

but something stopped you from sinking:
sewing, washing, sweeping, cooking, talking.

There was always the burn of the axe handle against palms.

You remember the final stitch on the binding of the quilt,
spreading it out on the table, admiring the hours
of rocking and stitching, the colors and cutting,
and how the red square in the middle whispered to the needle and thread.

That red as red as the raspberries in the jam jars.
When you lifted the last jar out,
the water roiled on,
furious and empty,
hissing and rumbling,
before it cooled its surface back to glass.

The sunlight gloried in the ruby jars on the table,
but had nothing to say.

Outside the window, the river,
muddily determined, kept passing by.

Inside the room you can't hear a sound.

Correspondence: Printed Receipt for a Funeral

—Seattle, Washington, May 17, 1908

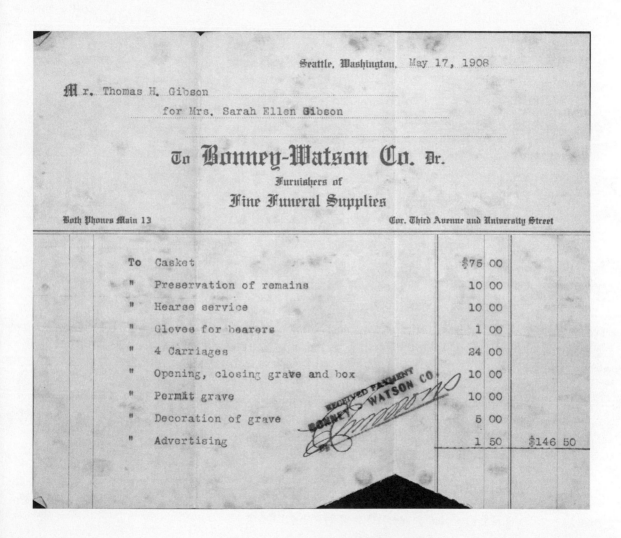

Seattle, Washington, May 17, 1908

Mr. Thomas H. Gibson

for Mrs. Sarah Ellen Gibson

To Bonney-Watson Co. Dr.

Furnishers of
Fine Funeral Supplies

Both Phones Main 13   Cor. Third Avenue and University Street

To	Casket	$75 00	
"	Preservation of remains	10 00	
"	Hearse service	10 00	
"	Gloves for bearers	1 00	
"	4 Carriages	24 00	
"	Opening, closing grave and box	10 00	
"	Permit grave	10 00	
"	Decoration of grave	5 00	
"	Advertising	1 50	$146 50

Son, of This, You and I Will Never Speak

Because you are my son, I will not
tell you about the moment you were
born, raw and wailing, into the burn

of the still July air. Mothers and
sons don't confess to pain like daughters
and mothers. Or that's what I assume.

I recall the shouting, my eyes screwed
tight against effort, the assistant
holding my knee, pushing her full weight

against me. I recall my right hand
rubbing my belly, feeling the knots
of your heels, even as you left

me. I recall the midwife, the bowl,
a damp cloth, a clink, the lace curtain.
If your father was waiting just then,

I didn't know. My world reduced
to your heels, my palm, the in-between,
and I paused to say good-bye to you,

knowing your departure was only
mine to witness. Then, my face tightened.
In silence, I went about the work

that was mine alone. With my effort
and her exhortations, you were born.
Of this, you and I will never speak.

Someday you might wait, boot soles on wood
slats, hands aching for work, but for your wife
that pause will be the whole world.

Notes

"Almost Anagram" Phyllis Movius noted the timing of Sarah Ellen Gibson's change of name in her book *A Place of Belonging.*

"Correspondence: A Recommendation" Sarah Ellen Gibson Collection, Box 1, Folder 2, Archives, Alaska and Polar Regions Collections, Rasmuson Library, University of Alaska Fairbanks.

"Chilkoot Trail" Joe's letters are taken from the letters he wrote to Sarah while she waited in San Francisco. Some parts of the poems break his words into found poems; others are my imaginings. Sarah's letters are invented responses. Sarah Ellen Gibson Collection, Box 1, Folders 8–12, Archives, Alaska and Polar Regions Collections, Rasmuson Library, University of Alaska Fairbanks. I owe a debt to Tappan Adney's descriptive details in his account of the Chilkoot Trail, *The Klondike Stampede of 1897–1898.* I'm especially grateful that Mr. Adney happened to be on the trail at the same time as Joe Gibson.

"At Last an Invitation from 13 Eldorado" is derived from a letter Joe wrote to Sarah. Sarah Ellen Gibson Collection, Box 1, Folder 14, Archives, Alaska and Polar Regions Collections, Rasmuson Library, University of Alaska Fairbanks.

"Correspondence: Receipt for Freight" Sarah Ellen Gibson Collection, Box 5, Folder 417, Archives, Alaska and Polar Regions Collections, Rasmuson Library, University of Alaska Fairbanks.

"On Dominion Creek Tom Makes a Decision" Thanks to Audrey Loftus's article, "Tom Gibson—Meat Hunter," which appeared in *Alaska Sportsman* in August 1967, for suggesting Tom's epiphany occurred here.

"Correspondence: Free Miner's Certificate" Sarah Ellen Gibson Collection, Box 5, Folder 422, Archives, Alaska and Polar Regions Collections, Rasmuson Library, University of Alaska Fairbanks.

"Tom Breaks Cargo on the Steamers" owes its existence (and some images) to Audrey Loftus's article "Tom Gibson—Meat Hunter."

"Correspondence: A Contract, Witnessed, Sealed, and Signed" Sarah Ellen Gibson Collection, Box 6, Folder 433, Archives, Alaska and Polar Regions Collections, Rasmuson Library, University of Alaska Fairbanks.

"Nellie Thinks She Should Have Waited for the Boat" Sarah Ellen Gibson Collection, Box 1, Folder 70, Archives, Alaska and Polar Regions Collections, Rasmuson Library, University of Alaska Fairbanks.

"Tom Makes a Narrow Escape" and "Tom and Elmer Dive for the Gun" contain some lines drawn from "Struggle in River: Dawson Men's Narrow Escape," which appeared in the *Dawson Daily News*, Saturday, May 30, 1903. Sarah Ellen Gibson Collection, Box 1, Folder 73, Archives, Alaska and Polar Regions Collections, Rasmuson Library, University of Alaska Fairbanks.

"Not Near as Wild" Sarah Ellen Gibson Collection, Box 1, Folder 73, Archives, Alaska and Polar Regions Collections, Rasmuson Library, University of Alaska Fairbanks.

"Elmer Considers the Old Man Drinking" Sarah Ellen Gibson Collection. Box 2, Folder 176, Archives, Alaska and Polar Regions Collections, Rasmuson Library, University of Alaska Fairbanks.

"Tom Returns to Dawson" Sarah Ellen Gibson Collection, Box 2, Folder 116, Archives, Alaska and Polar Regions Collections, Rasmuson Library, University of Alaska Fairbanks.

"Luck Conspires against Tom and Elmer" owes its existence to Audrey Loftus's article "Tom Gibson—Meat Hunter."

"Correspondence: Handwritten Receipt" Sarah Ellen Gibson Collection, Box 5, Folder 419, Archives, Alaska and Polar Regions Collections, Rasmuson Library, University of Alaska Fairbanks.

"Mother-in-law" Sarah Ellen Gibson Collection, Box 2, Folder 176, Archives, Alaska and Polar Regions Collections, Rasmuson Library, University of Alaska Fairbanks.

"Correspondence: A Letter From Madame M. Yale" and "Correspondence: An Unanswered Questionnaire Tucked in a Packet of Letters" Sarah Ellen Gibson Collection, Box 2, Folder 169, Archives, Alaska and Polar Regions Collections, Rasmuson Library, University of Alaska Fairbanks.

"Correspondence: A Note on a Prescription Pad" Sarah Ellen Gibson Collection, Box 3, Folder 225, Archives, Alaska and Polar Regions Collections, Rasmuson Library, University of Alaska Fairbanks.

"Until Payment Can't Be Made" Sarah Ellen Gibson Collection, Box 4, Folder 278, Box 3, Folder 215, Archives, Alaska and Polar Regions Collections, Rasmuson Library, University of Alaska Fairbanks.

"Correspondence: Printed Receipt for a Funeral" Sarah Ellen Gibson Collection, Box 5, Folder 418, Archives, Alaska and Polar Regions Collections, Rasmuson Library, University of Alaska Fairbanks.

Biographical Note

Nicole Stellon O'Donnell's poems have appeared in *Prairie Schooner, Beloit Poetry Journal, The Women's Review of Books, Ice Floe, Cirque,* and other literary journals. She received an Individual Artist Award from the Rasmuson Foundation to support the writing of *Steam Laundry*. She lives, writes, and teaches in Fairbanks, Alaska.